WELCOME TO THE U.S.A.
IOWA

Written by Ann Heinrichs   Illustrated by Matt Kania
Content Adviser: Dorothy A. Schwieder, University Professor
Emeritus of History, Iowa State University, Ames, Iowa

The Child's World

Published in the United States of America by The Child's World®
PO Box 326 • Chanhassen, MN 55317-0326
800-599-READ • www.childsworld.com

Photo Credits
Cover: Getty Images/The Image Bank/Pete Turner; frontispiece: Iowa Tourism Office.

Interior: AP/Wide World Photo: 13 (Waterloo Courier/Brandon Pollock), 14 (Telegraph Herald/Joseph A. Wallis), 18 (The Hawk Eye/Scott Morgan), 30 (Mason City Globe-Gazette/Arian Schuessler); Corbis: 9 (Tom Bean), 10 (Julie Habel), 21 (Buddy Mays), 25 (Annie Griffiths Belt), 29 (Craig Aurness); Iowa Tourism Office: 22, 26, 33; Macerich Management Company/Southern Hills Mall: 17; Erik Utterback: 6; Wells' Dairy: 34.

Acknowledgments
The Child's World®: Mary Berendes, Publishing Director

Editorial Directions, Inc.: E. Russell Primm, Editorial Director; Katie Marsico, Associate Editor; Judith Shiffer, Assistant Editor; Matt Messbarger, Editorial Assistant; Susan Hindman, Copy Editor; Melissa McDaniel, Proofreader; Kevin Cunningham, Peter Garnham, Matt Messbarger, Olivia Nellums, Chris Simms, Molly Symmonds, Katherine Trickle, Carl Stephen Wender, Fact Checkers; Tim Griffin/IndexServ, Indexer; Cian Loughlin O'Day, Photo Researcher and Editor

The Design Lab: Kathleen Petelinsek, Design; Julia Goozen, Art Production

Library of Congress Cataloging-in-Publication Data
Heinrichs, Ann.
  Iowa / by Ann Heinrichs ; cartography and illustrations by Matt Kania.
    p. cm. — (Welcome to the U.S.A.)
  Includes index.
  ISBN 1-59296-473-7 (library bound : alk. paper) 1. Iowa—Juvenile literature. I. Kania, Matt, ill. II. Title.
  F621.3.H455 2005
  977.7—dc22
                                                2005015381

Ann Heinrichs is the author of more than 100 books for children and young adults. She has also enjoyed successful careers as a children's book editor and an advertising copywriter. Ann grew up in Fort Smith, Arkansas, and lives in Chicago, Illinois.

About the Author
Ann Heinrichs

Matt Kania loves maps and, as a kid, dreamed of making them. In school he studied geography and cartography, and today he makes maps for a living. Matt's favorite thing about drawing maps is learning about the places they represent. Many of the maps he has created can be found in books, magazines, videos, Web sites, and public places.

About the
Map Illustrator
Matt Kania

On the cover: Want to learn about farming? Iowa's the state for you!
On page one: All aboard! Ride a train through scenic Boone Valley.

OUR IOWA TRIP

Shall we take a trip through Iowa today? You'll find it's a great place to explore. Here's just a taste of what's to come.

You'll ride your bike through the countryside. You'll watch wildlife and explore caves. You'll see huge earthen mounds shaped like animals. You'll gaze upon miles of leafy cornfields. You'll learn about old-time farm life. You'll watch windmills on a wind farm. You'll see how tractors and ice cream are made. And you'll meet some champion hogs!

Are you ready to roll? Then buckle up and hang on tight. We're off to discover Iowa!

WELCOME TO IOWA

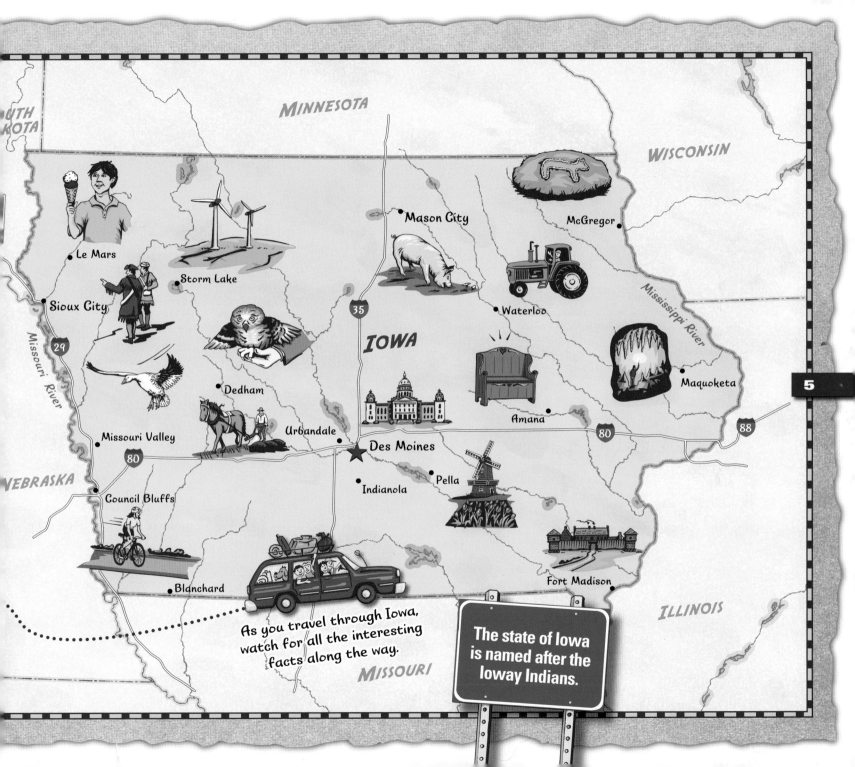

MINNESOTA

WISCONSIN

SOUTH DAKOTA

Le Mars

Sioux City

Storm Lake

Mason City

McGregor

Waterloo

Mississippi River

IOWA

Maquoketa

Dedham

Missouri River

Missouri Valley

Urbandale

Des Moines

Amana

Indianola

Pella

Council Bluffs

Blanchard

Fort Madison

NEBRASKA

MISSOURI

ILLINOIS

As you travel through Iowa, watch for all the interesting facts along the way.

The state of Iowa is named after the Ioway Indians.

Maquoketa Caves State Park

Grab your flashlight! Explore Maquoketa Caves State Park.

Wander through Dancehall Cave or Dugout Cave. Glistening rock formations are everywhere. You're exploring Maquoketa Caves State Park! It's in eastern Iowa near Maquoketa.

Prairies and rolling hills cover most of Iowa. The state lies between two big rivers. The Mississippi River forms the eastern border. Cliffs and rugged hills rise in the northeast.

The Missouri River outlines most of the western border. Tall **bluffs** overlook this river. The Des Moines River cuts through central Iowa. It flows from northwest to southeast. Then it enters the Mississippi River at Keokuk.

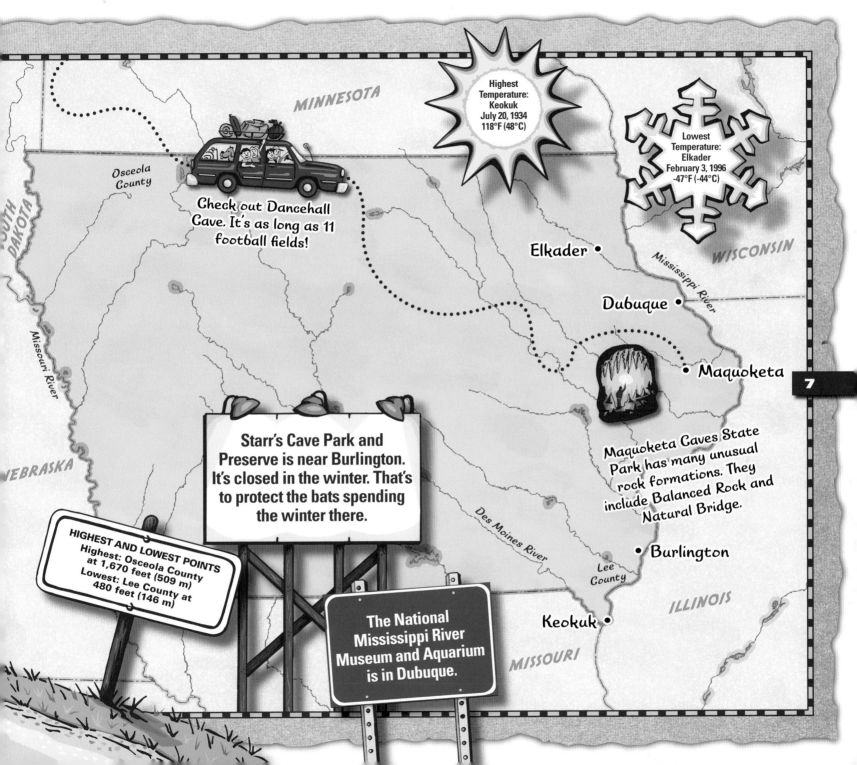

MINNESOTA

SOUTH DAKOTA

Osceola County

Check out Dancehall Cave. It's as long as 11 football fields!

Highest Temperature: Keokuk July 20, 1934 118°F (48°C)

Lowest Temperature: Elkader February 3, 1996 -47°F (-44°C)

WISCONSIN

Elkader •

Dubuque •

Mississippi River

Maquoketa •

Missouri River

NEBRASKA

Starr's Cave Park and Preserve is near Burlington. It's closed in the winter. That's to protect the bats spending the winter there.

Maquoketa Caves State Park has many unusual rock formations. They include Balanced Rock and Natural Bridge.

Des Moines River

HIGHEST AND LOWEST POINTS
Highest: Osceola County at 1,670 feet (509 m)
Lowest: Lee County at 480 feet (146 m)

• Burlington

Lee County

ILLINOIS

The National Mississippi River Museum and Aquarium is in Dubuque.

Keokuk •

MISSOURI

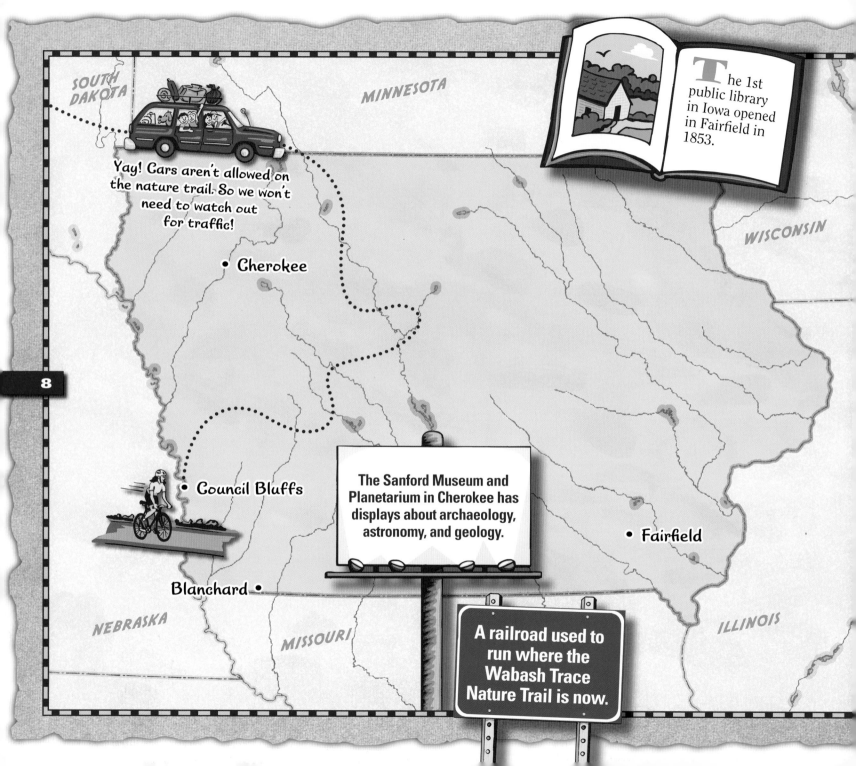

SOUTH DAKOTA

MINNESOTA

WISCONSIN

Yay! Cars aren't allowed on the nature trail. So we won't need to watch out for traffic!

The 1st public library in Iowa opened in Fairfield in 1853.

• Cherokee

• Council Bluffs

The Sanford Museum and Planetarium in Cherokee has displays about archaeology, astronomy, and geology.

• Fairfield

Blanchard •

NEBRASKA

MISSOURI

ILLINOIS

A railroad used to run where the Wabash Trace Nature Trail is now.

Biking the Wabash Trace Nature Trail

Do you like bike riding? Try biking the Wabash Trace Nature Trail. It stretches from Council Bluffs to Blanchard. Your path passes steep, sharply curving hills. It passes farms and villages. And it winds through leafy forests. Tree branches seem to form a shelter around you. You feel like you're in a green tunnel!

Biking is a favorite outdoor activity in Iowa. It's one of many ways to enjoy nature. Camping, boating, fishing, and swimming are popular, too. Some people like hiking in northeastern Iowa. Climbing those rugged hills is quite a workout!

Pedal faster! Tour Wabash Trace Nature Trail by bike.

Iowa artist Grant Wood painted many scenes of Iowa farm life.

The Neal Smith National Wildlife Refuge is near Prairie City. A herd of bison, or buffalo, lives there.

This fawn calls DeSoto National Wildlife Refuge home.

DeSoto National Wildlife Refuge continues west into Nebraska.

DeSoto National Wildlife Refuge

Want to watch animals in their natural homes? Then explore DeSoto National Wildlife Refuge. It's in western Iowa near Missouri Valley.

In the fall, many **migrating** waterbirds pass through. That includes about half a million snow geese! You'll also see deer in the refuge. In the summer, they're caring for newborn fawns.

Watch for cottontail rabbits, too. They hop through the brush and nibble plants. You may see a raccoon in a hollow log. Its furry little face has a black mask. And look out for opossums. They can hang from branches by their tails!

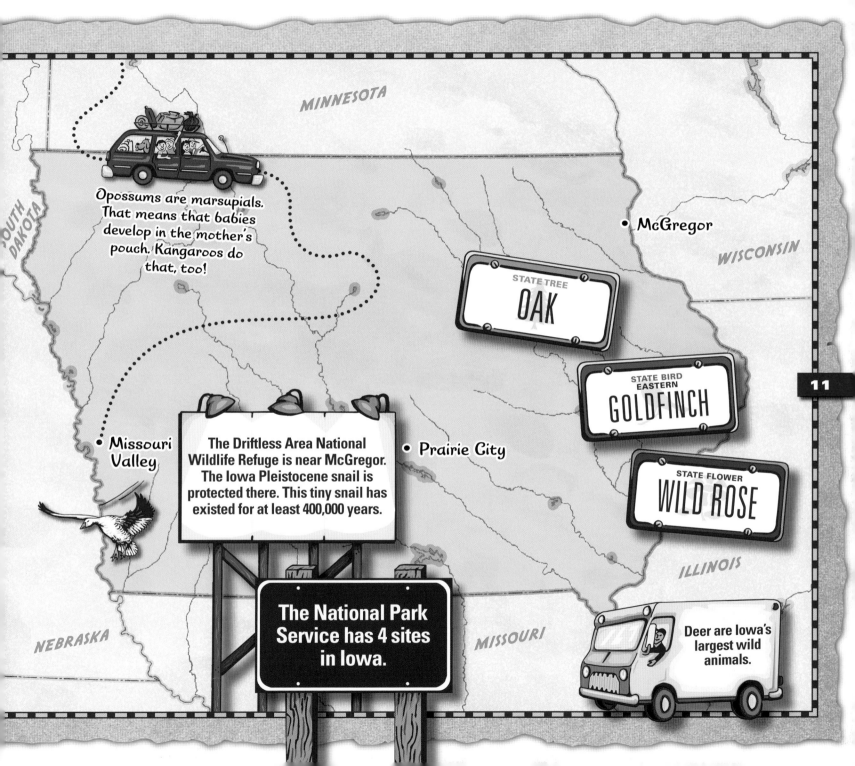

MINNESOTA

• McGregor

WISCONSIN

Opossums are marsupials. That means that babies develop in the mother's pouch. Kangaroos do that, too!

STATE TREE
OAK

STATE BIRD
EASTERN
GOLDFINCH

SOUTH DAKOTA

• Missouri Valley

The Driftless Area National Wildlife Refuge is near McGregor. The Iowa Pleistocene snail is protected there. This tiny snail has existed for at least 400,000 years.

• Prairie City

STATE FLOWER
WILD ROSE

ILLINOIS

The National Park Service has 4 sites in Iowa.

NEBRASKA

MISSOURI

Deer are Iowa's largest wild animals.

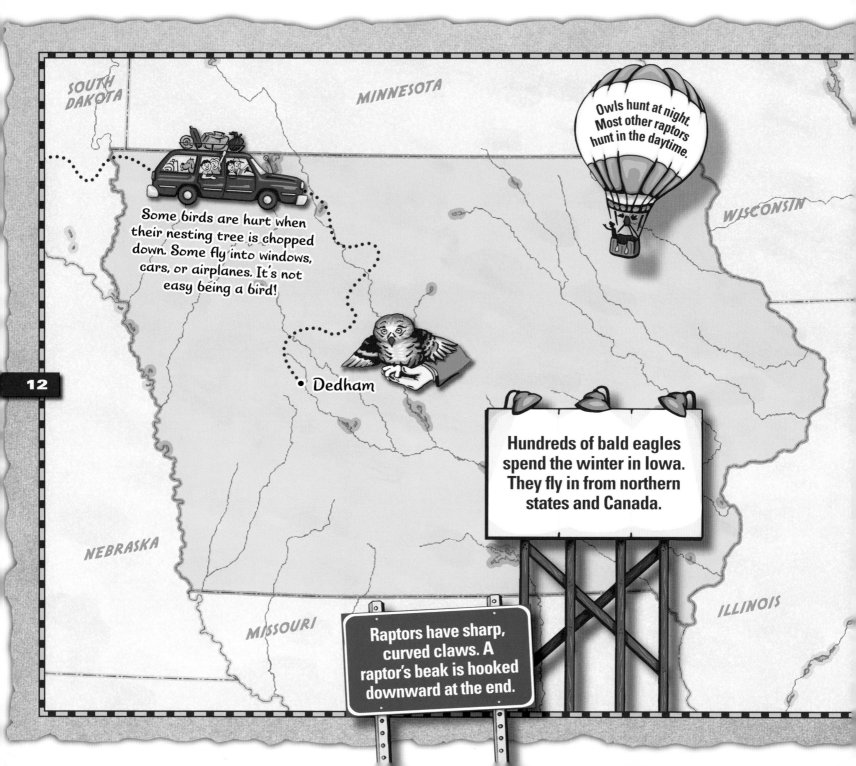

Owls hunt at night. Most other raptors hunt in the daytime.

Some birds are hurt when their nesting tree is chopped down. Some fly into windows, cars, or airplanes. It's not easy being a bird!

Hundreds of bald eagles spend the winter in Iowa. They fly in from northern states and Canada.

Raptors have sharp, curved claws. A raptor's beak is hooked downward at the end.

• Dedham

SOUTH DAKOTA

MINNESOTA

WISCONSIN

NEBRASKA

MISSOURI

ILLINOIS

Doctoring Birds in Dedham

Birds can get hurt in many ways. That's why Saving Our **Avian** Resources was founded. It's called SOAR for short. This organization takes in injured birds. It gives them medical care. The birds stay until they're well. Then they're released into the wild again.

You can visit SOAR in Dedham. Walk through and meet the feathered patients. They may have a broken leg or wing. But they can safely heal here.

Most of SOAR's patients are raptors. Those are birds that hunt animals for food. They include hawks, owls, eagles, and falcons.

SOAR is helping this injured owl recover.

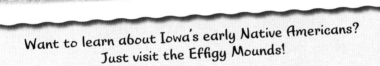

Want to learn about Iowa's early Native Americans?
Just visit the Effigy Mounds!

Effigy Mounds includes about 200 mounds. About 30 of them are shaped like animals.

Effigy Mounds National Monument

First, you think you're seeing hills.

But get a little closer. The hills form shapes and patterns. They're shaped like bears, birds, and other figures!

These hills are the **Effigy** Mounds near McGregor. Early Indians built them hundreds of years ago. The mounds may have had religious purposes.

French explorers from Canada arrived in 1673. They were Louis Jolliet and Father Jacques Marquette. They came down the Mississippi River in canoes. Soon fur traders moved into the region. They met several Native American groups. Some raised crops in the rich soil. Others hunted buffalo across the prairies.

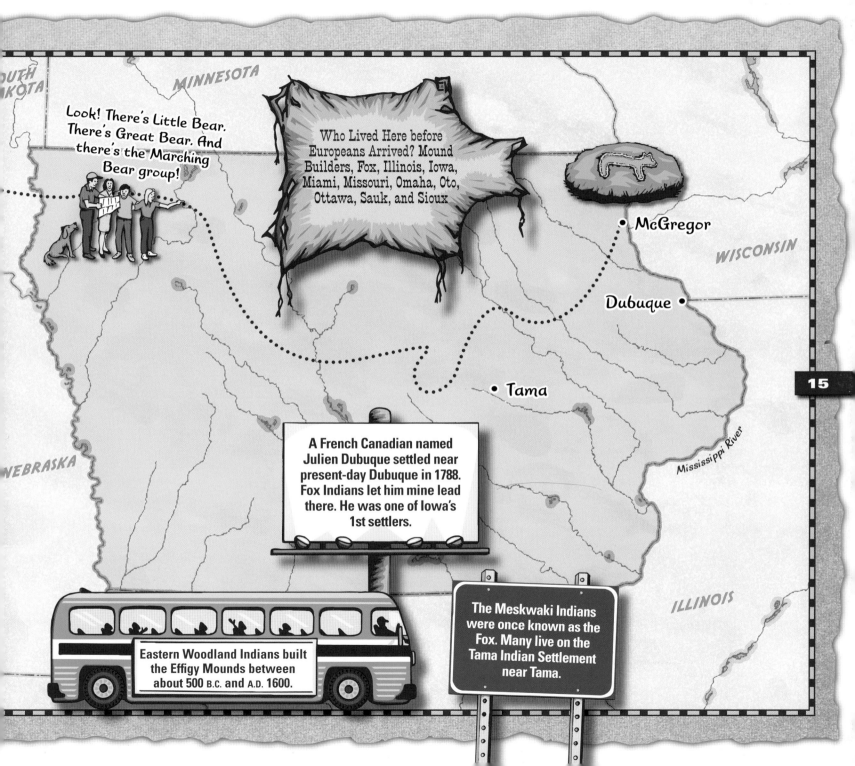

Look! There's Little Bear. There's Great Bear. And there's the Marching Bear group!

Who Lived Here before Europeans Arrived? Mound Builders, Fox, Illinois, Iowa, Miami, Missouri, Omaha, Oto, Ottawa, Sauk, and Sioux

A French Canadian named Julien Dubuque settled near present-day Dubuque in 1788. Fox Indians let him mine lead there. He was one of Iowa's 1st settlers.

The Meskwaki Indians were once known as the Fox. Many live on the Tama Indian Settlement near Tama.

Eastern Woodland Indians built the Effigy Mounds between about 500 B.C. and A.D. 1600.

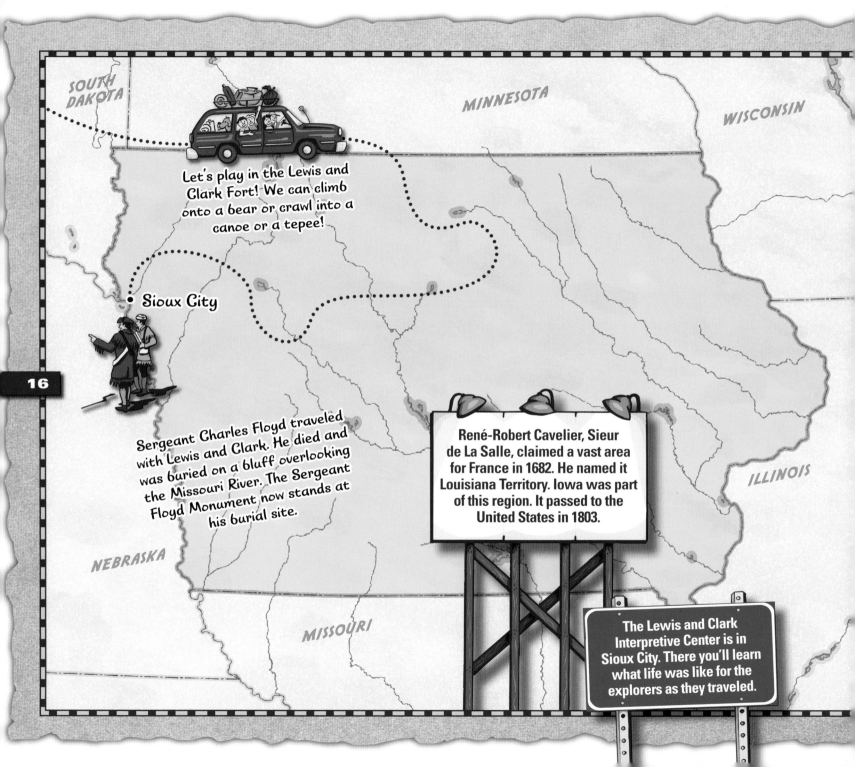

Let's play in the Lewis and Clark Fort! We can climb onto a bear or crawl into a canoe or a tepee!

SOUTH DAKOTA

MINNESOTA

WISCONSIN

• Sioux City

Sergeant Charles Floyd traveled with Lewis and Clark. He died and was buried on a bluff overlooking the Missouri River. The Sergeant Floyd Monument now stands at his burial site.

René-Robert Cavelier, Sieur de La Salle, claimed a vast area for France in 1682. He named it Louisiana Territory. Iowa was part of this region. It passed to the United States in 1803.

ILLINOIS

NEBRASKA

MISSOURI

The Lewis and Clark Interpretive Center is in Sioux City. There you'll learn what life was like for the explorers as they traveled.

Lewis and Clark at the Mall

Drop by Southern Hills Mall in Sioux City. Above the shops are thirty-eight huge paintings. They show scenes of a famous journey. It was led by Meriwether Lewis and William Clark.

These explorers passed along Iowa's western border in 1804. They hoped to reach the Pacific Ocean. And they did! They returned along Iowa's western border in 1806.

Lewis and Clark met many Indians along the way. They mapped rivers and studied animals, too. They built camps and forts for shelter.

Check out the mall's Lewis and Clark Fort. It's a play area for kids. You can do lots of exploring there!

What was Lewis and Clark's journey like? See for yourself at Southern Hills Mall!

The U.S. Congress created the Territory of Iowa in 1838.

Old Fort Madison

Ready, aim, fire! You're touring Old Fort Madison.

Wander through the log buildings. People in old-fashioned costumes greet you. Join them as they dip candles or bake. Or try lifting a heavy **musket.** This is how soldiers and their families lived. You're visiting Old Fort Madison!

U.S. Army soldiers built Fort Madison in 1808. It protected a nearby fur-trading post.

The U.S. government began moving Indians off their land. Some were moved from Illinois into Iowa. But Sauk chief Black Hawk didn't want to move. The army fought him and his followers in 1832. This is called the Black Hawk War. The Indians lost and had to move.

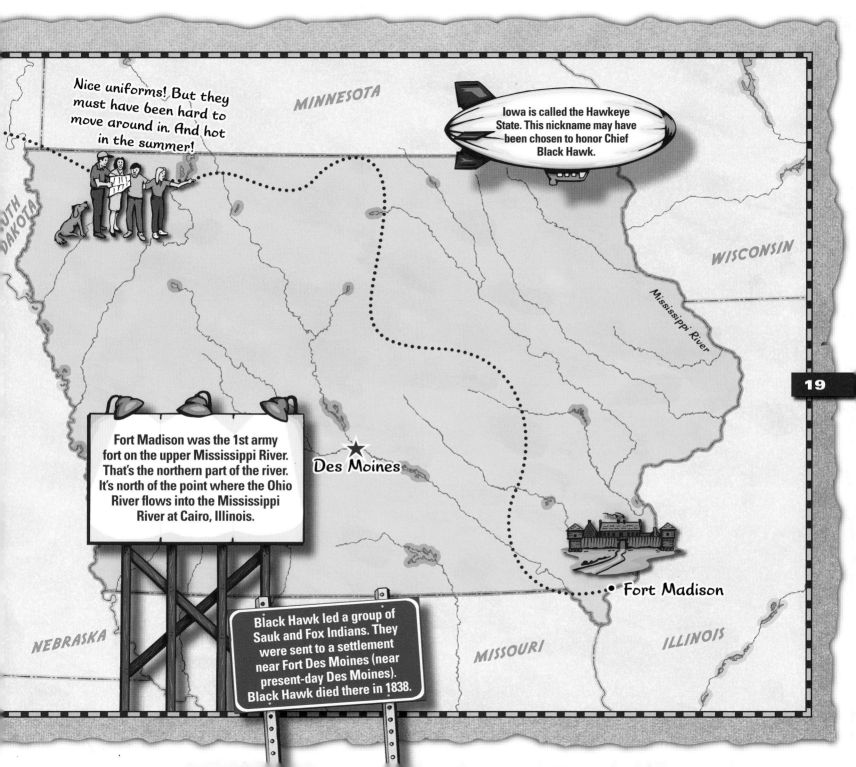

Nice uniforms! But they must have been hard to move around in. And hot in the summer!

Iowa is called the Hawkeye State. This nickname may have been chosen to honor Chief Black Hawk.

Fort Madison was the 1st army fort on the upper Mississippi River. That's the northern part of the river. It's north of the point where the Ohio River flows into the Mississippi River at Cairo, Illinois.

★ Des Moines

• Fort Madison

Black Hawk led a group of Sauk and Fox Indians. They were sent to a settlement near Fort Des Moines (near present-day Des Moines). Black Hawk died there in 1838.

MINNESOTA

SOUTH DAKOTA

WISCONSIN

Mississippi River

NEBRASKA

MISSOURI

ILLINOIS

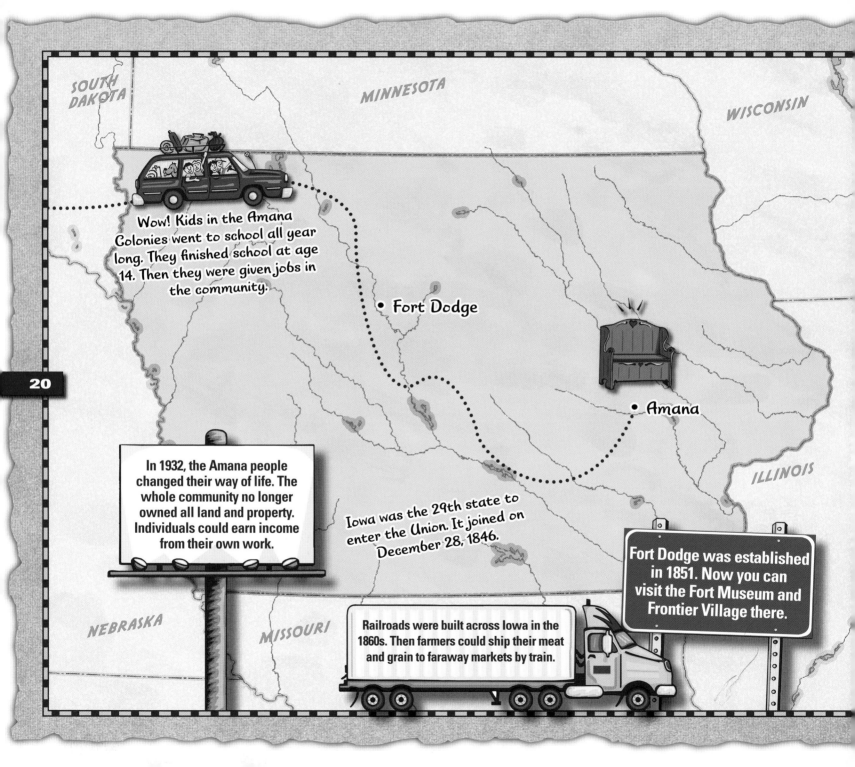

SOUTH DAKOTA

MINNESOTA

WISCONSIN

Wow! Kids in the Amana Colonies went to school all year long. They finished school at age 14. Then they were given jobs in the community.

• Fort Dodge

• Amana

ILLINOIS

In 1932, the Amana people changed their way of life. The whole community no longer owned all land and property. Individuals could earn income from their own work.

Iowa was the 29th state to enter the Union. It joined on December 28, 1846.

Fort Dodge was established in 1851. Now you can visit the Fort Museum and Frontier Village there.

NEBRASKA

MISSOURI

Railroads were built across Iowa in the 1860s. Then farmers could ship their meat and grain to faraway markets by train.

The Amana Colonies

See the old barns, bakeries, churches, and schools. Then browse through the shops. You'll see workers making furniture and woolen goods. You're at the Amana **Colonies**!

By the 1850s, settlers were pouring into Iowa. Many were **immigrants.** One group was the Amana Society. They left Germany seeking religious freedom. They founded their first Iowa village in 1855.

The Amana Society believed in sharing. All land and buildings belonged to the group. Each person had special tasks. They worked in kitchens, fields, or shops. Amana goods became known for their high quality.

Yikes! That's hot! A blacksmith works with metal at the Amana Colonies.

The Amana community built 7 villages in east-central Iowa.

The Danish Immigrant Museum is in Elk Horn. Danish people are from Denmark.

Pella's Tulip Time Festival

Try some *vetbollen*. They're deep-fried apple pastries. Watch the dancers in their *klompen*. Those are **traditional** Dutch wooden shoes. Then look all around town. You see thousands of tulips in bloom. You're at the Pella Tulip Time Festival!

This festival celebrates Dutch **heritage.** Many Dutch immigrants settled around Pella. The Dutch are people from the Netherlands. This country is famous for growing tulips. So people in Pella planted tulips, too.

Many other immigrants came to Iowa. They all made new homes there. Many of these groups hold festivals today.

Are tulips your favorite flower? Check out Pella's Tulip Time Festival.

Both Pella and Orange City hold tulip festivals.

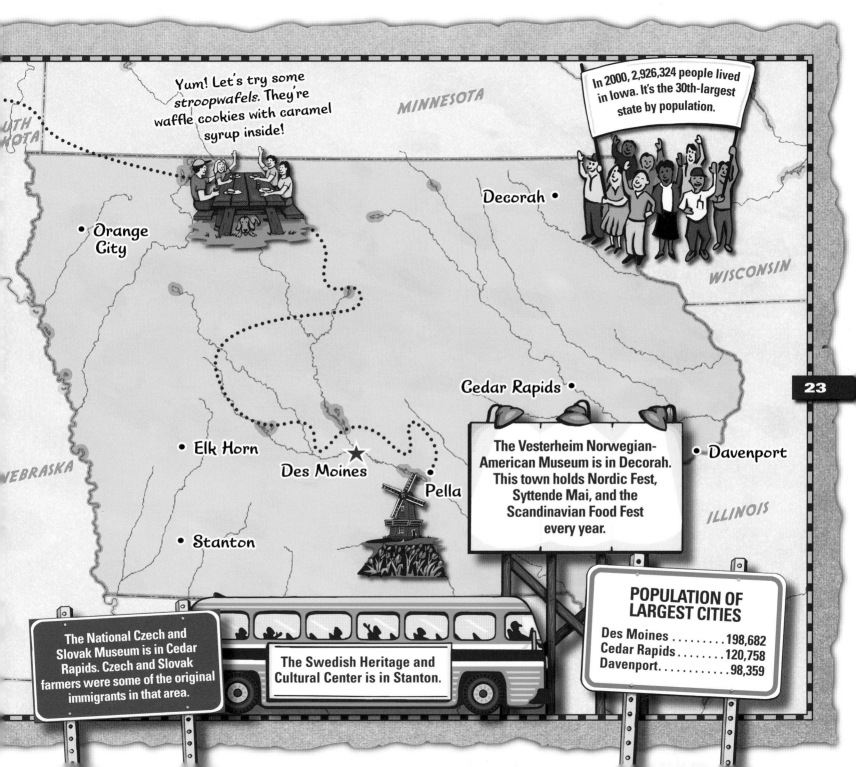

Yum! Let's try some *stroopwafels*. They're waffle cookies with caramel syrup inside!

MINNESOTA

In 2000, 2,926,324 people lived in Iowa. It's the 30th-largest state by population.

SOUTH DAKOTA

Decorah •

• Orange City

WISCONSIN

Cedar Rapids •

The Vesterheim Norwegian-American Museum is in Decorah. This town holds Nordic Fest, Syttende Mai, and the Scandinavian Food Fest every year.

• Davenport

• Elk Horn

Des Moines

Pella

NEBRASKA

ILLINOIS

• Stanton

The National Czech and Slovak Museum is in Cedar Rapids. Czech and Slovak farmers were some of the original immigrants in that area.

The Swedish Heritage and Cultural Center is in Stanton.

POPULATION OF LARGEST CITIES

Des Moines 198,682
Cedar Rapids 120,758
Davenport 98,359

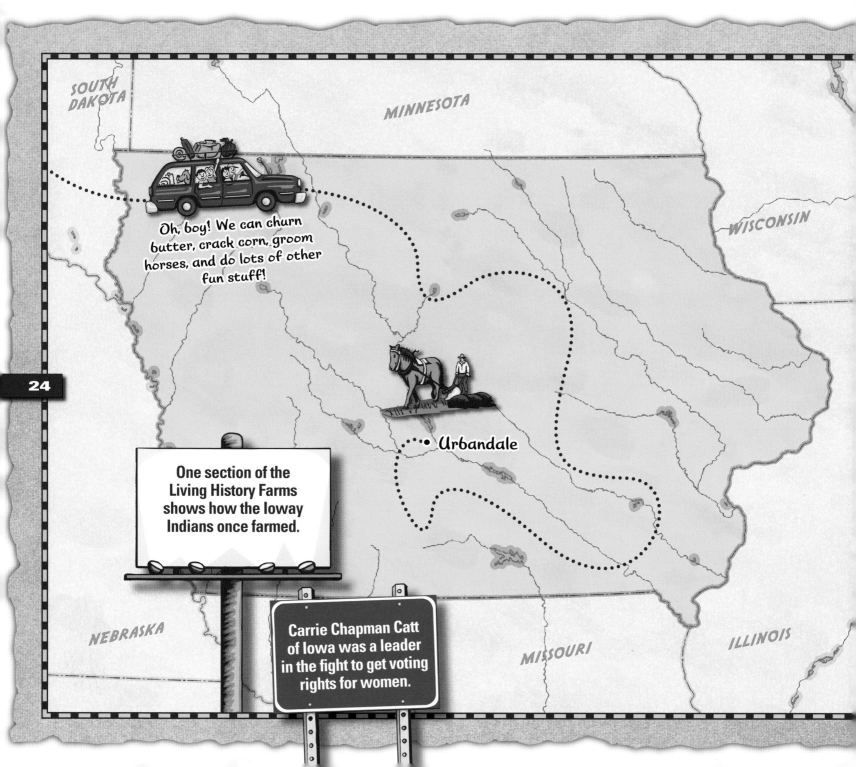

Oh, boy! We can churn butter, crack corn, groom horses, and do lots of other fun stuff!

• Urbandale

One section of the Living History Farms shows how the Ioway Indians once farmed.

Carrie Chapman Catt of Iowa was a leader in the fight to get voting rights for women.

How did Iowa life change over the years? Just visit the Living History Farms in Urbandale. You'll see communities from four periods in time. A tractor pulls you from one to the other!

Suppose you lived in Iowa about 1875. You might have visited towns such as Walnut Hill. It's built as a bustling frontier town. You'll see merchants and craftspeople there. They offered services for the region's farmers.

You'll also visit a farm from about 1900. Farmers had many machines by then. Some machines mowed hay or planted corn. Others tied crops into bundles. Horses pulled these machines along.

Have you ever shucked corn? Give it a try at the Living History Farms!

One of the Living History Farms is an 1850s pioneer farm.

Check out all the rides and games! There's plenty to do at the Iowa State Fair!

Webster City holds the Raspberry Festival every year. The world's largest raspberry dessert is served there!

Mason City's North Iowa Fair

See who wins the tallest-cornstalk contest. Check out a horse show. Or watch people roping cattle. Then catch the hog show. You won't believe how big hogs can grow!

You're enjoying Mason City's North Iowa Fair. Many Iowa cities hold farm fairs. The biggest fair is the Iowa State Fair. It's held in Des Moines every year.

Farms cover most of Iowa. Corn is the state's leading crop. Soybeans are an important crop, too.

What becomes of the corn and soybeans? Hogs and cattle eat a lot of these crops. Iowa raises more hogs than any other state!

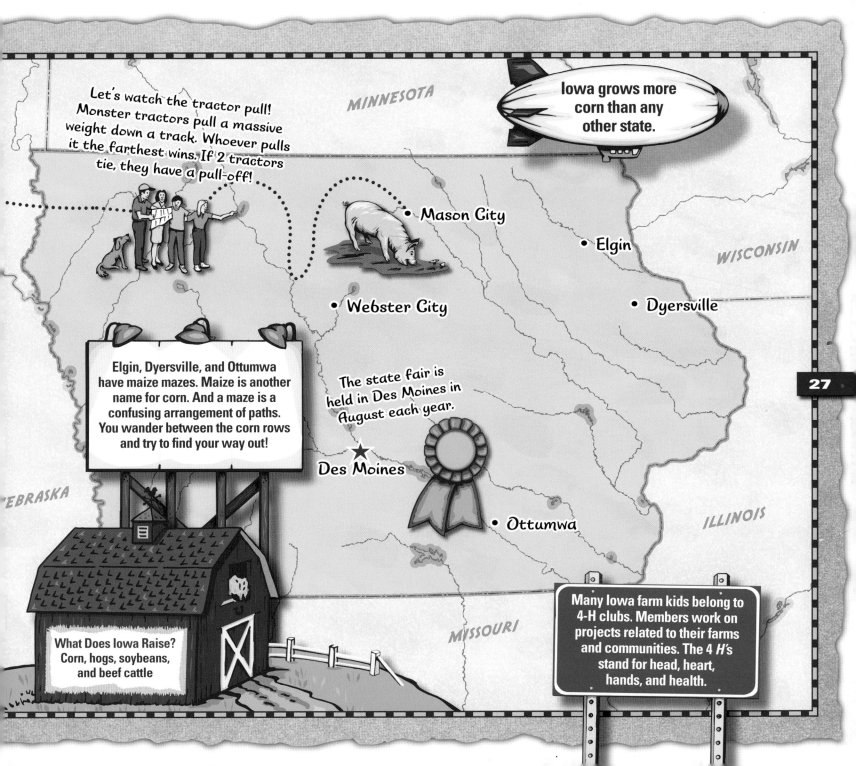

Let's watch the tractor pull! Monster tractors pull a massive weight down a track. Whoever pulls it the farthest wins. If 2 tractors tie, they have a pull-off!

Iowa grows more corn than any other state.

MINNESOTA

WISCONSIN

• Mason City

• Elgin

• Webster City

• Dyersville

Elgin, Dyersville, and Ottumwa have maize mazes. Maize is another name for corn. And a maze is a confusing arrangement of paths. You wander between the corn rows and try to find your way out!

The state fair is held in Des Moines in August each year.

★ Des Moines

NEBRASKA

ILLINOIS

• Ottumwa

MISSOURI

What Does Iowa Raise? Corn, hogs, soybeans, and beef cattle

Many Iowa farm kids belong to 4-H clubs. Members work on projects related to their farms and communities. The 4 H's stand for head, heart, hands, and health.

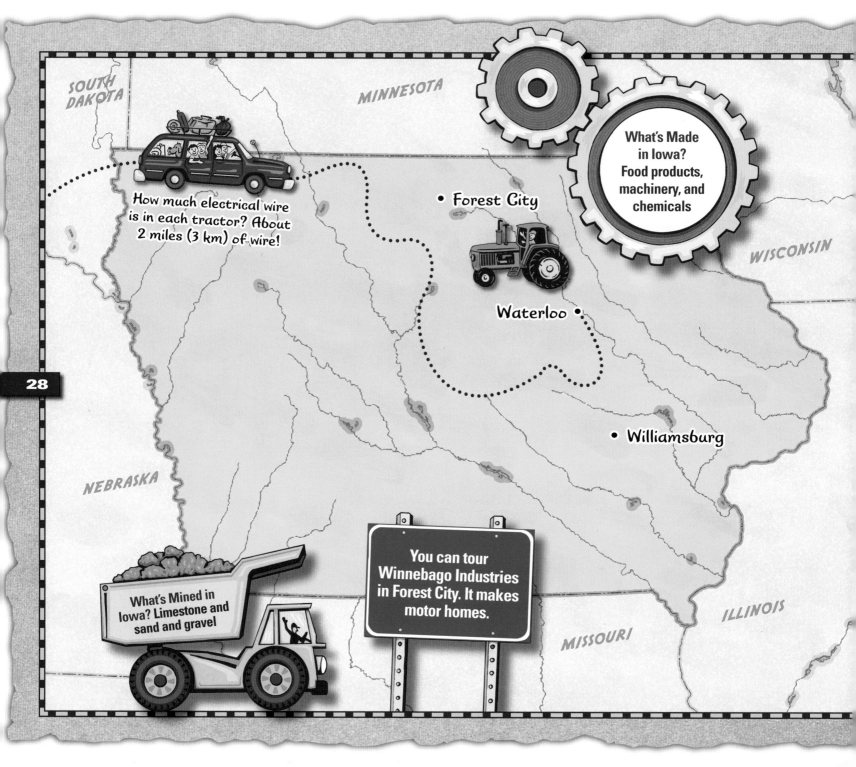

SOUTH DAKOTA

MINNESOTA

WISCONSIN

NEBRASKA

ILLINOIS

MISSOURI

How much electrical wire is in each tractor? About 2 miles (3 km) of wire!

• Forest City

Waterloo •

• Williamsburg

What's Made in Iowa? Food products, machinery, and chemicals

What's Mined in Iowa? Limestone and sand and gravel

You can tour Winnebago Industries in Forest City. It makes motor homes.

The John Deere Tractor Factory in Waterloo

Make sure you're wearing closed-toed shoes. Your toes might not be safe in sandals. Then hop on the tour cart. You'll zoom all over the John Deere Tractor Factory. There you'll see how big, green tractors are made!

Farm machinery is an important Iowa product. Some factories make construction machinery, too. But foods are Iowa's top factory goods. Some food plants process and package meat. They might make hogs into ham or sausage. Other food plants process crops. Take corn, for example. It's made into corn oil or cornmeal. And don't forget another great corn product—popcorn!

Ever wonder how tractors are made? Tour the John Deere factory and find out!

The Kinze Manufacturing plant in Williamsburg builds planting equipment and grain wagons.

Buena Vista County Wind Farm

Head out to Buffalo Ridge near Storm Lake. You'll see rows of huge, three-armed windmills. You've found the Buena Vista County Wind Farm!

In the twentieth century, Iowans looked toward the future. They saw the country faced energy problems. Oil, gas, and coal are common energy sources. But they release harmful materials into the **environment.** These sources won't last forever, either. And when supplies are low, energy prices soar.

Some Iowans decided to create electricity with wind power. Wind is clean, and it doesn't run out. Wind turns the wind farm's windmills. And that creates electricity for thousands of homes.

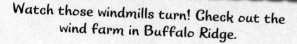

Watch those windmills turn! Check out the wind farm in Buffalo Ridge.

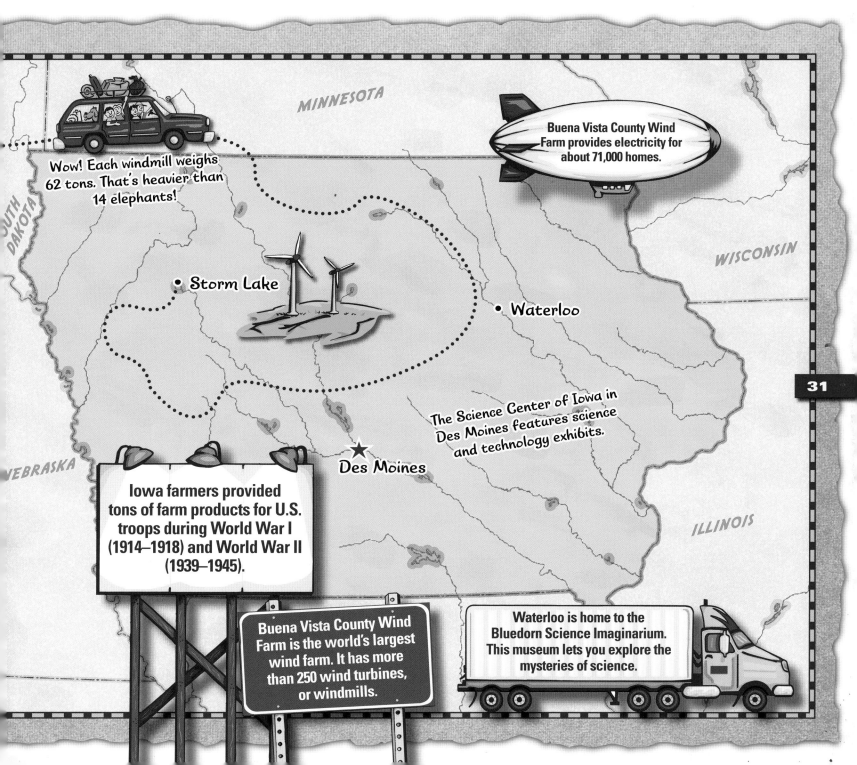

Wow! Each windmill weighs 62 tons. That's heavier than 14 elephants!

MINNESOTA

Buena Vista County Wind Farm provides electricity for about 71,000 homes.

SOUTH DAKOTA

WISCONSIN

• Storm Lake

• Waterloo

The Science Center of Iowa in Des Moines features science and technology exhibits.

★ Des Moines

NEBRASKA

Iowa farmers provided tons of farm products for U.S. troops during World War I (1914–1918) and World War II (1939–1945).

ILLINOIS

Buena Vista County Wind Farm is the world's largest wind farm. It has more than 250 wind turbines, or windmills.

Waterloo is home to the Bluedorn Science Imaginarium. This museum lets you explore the mysteries of science.

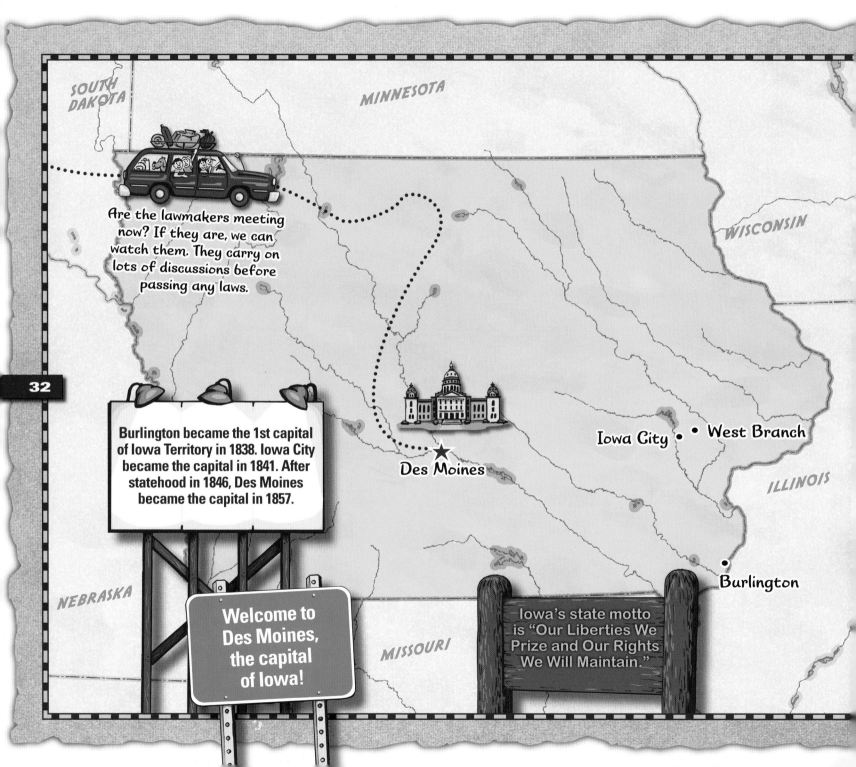

Are the lawmakers meeting now? If they are, we can watch them. They carry on lots of discussions before passing any laws.

Burlington became the 1st capital of Iowa Territory in 1838. Iowa City became the capital in 1841. After statehood in 1846, Des Moines became the capital in 1857.

Welcome to Des Moines, the capital of Iowa!

Iowa's state motto is "Our Liberties We Prize and Our Rights We Will Maintain."

SOUTH DAKOTA

MINNESOTA

WISCONSIN

NEBRASKA

MISSOURI

ILLINOIS

Des Moines

Iowa City • • West Branch

• Burlington

The State Capitol in Des Moines

You'll know when you're in Des Moines. Just look across the skyline. You'll see something golden glistening in the sun. It's the state capitol's big, rounded dome!

Inside this grand building are state government offices. Iowa has three branches of government. One branch makes the state's laws. Its members belong to Iowa's General Assembly. The governor heads another branch. It enforces, or carries out, the laws. The third branch is made up of judges. They apply the laws. That means they listen to cases in courts. Then they decide if someone has broken the law.

Lawmakers are hard at work inside Iowa's capitol.

Herbert Hoover was the 31st president (1929–1933). He was born in West Branch.

The Ice Cream Capital of the World

34

What's your favorite flavor of ice cream? Try a few samples at Wells' Dairy!

Do you like ice cream? Then visit Wells' Dairy in Le Mars. No spot in the world makes more ice cream!

Iowa's General Assembly decided to honor Le Mars. It gave the city a delicious-sounding nickname. Can you guess what that nickname is? The Ice Cream Capital of the World!

Drop by the dairy's visitor's center. There you'll see how ice cream is made. You'll even stroll through an ice cream museum. And don't miss the ice cream parlor. There you'll enjoy some great treats!

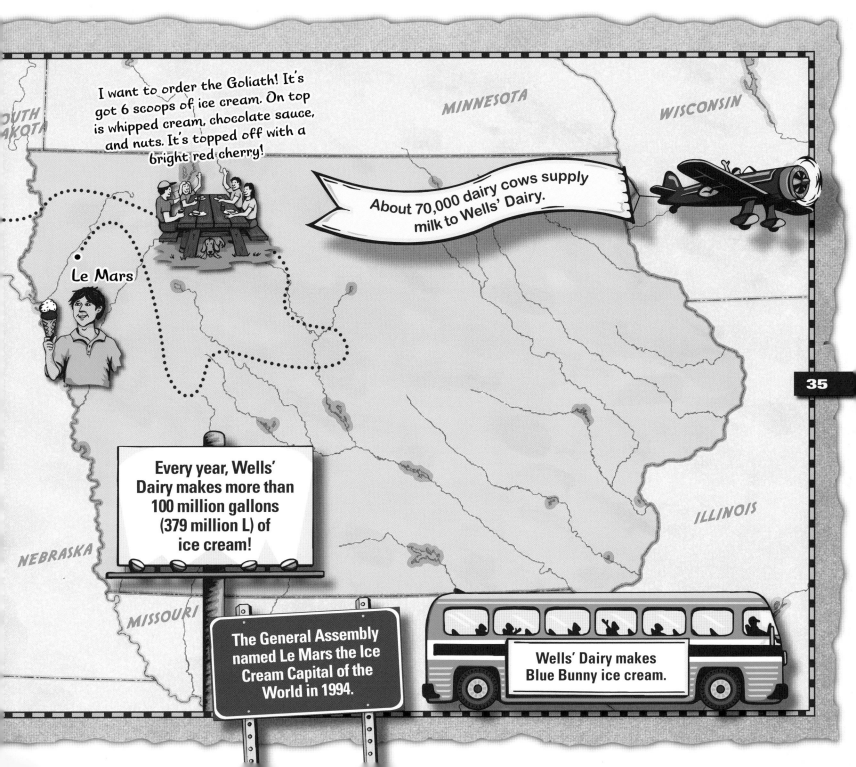

I want to order the Goliath! It's got 6 scoops of ice cream. On top is whipped cream, chocolate sauce, and nuts. It's topped off with a bright red cherry!

Le Mars

About 70,000 dairy cows supply milk to Wells' Dairy.

Every year, Wells' Dairy makes more than 100 million gallons (379 million L) of ice cream!

The General Assembly named Le Mars the Ice Cream Capital of the World in 1994.

Wells' Dairy makes Blue Bunny ice cream.

SOUTH DAKOTA

MINNESOTA

WISCONSIN

NEBRASKA

MISSOURI

ILLINOIS

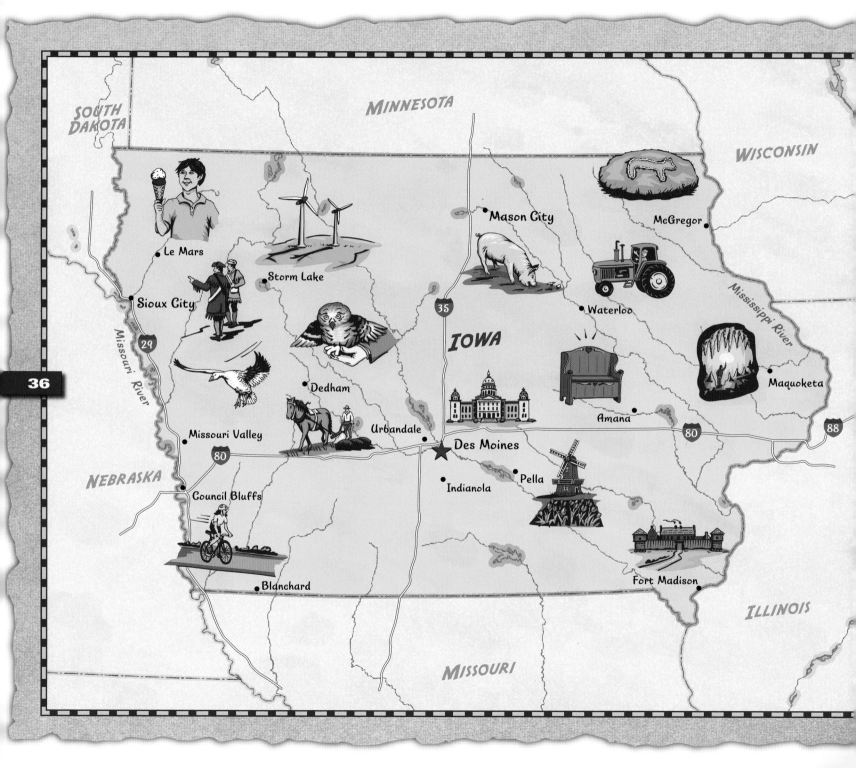

SOUTH DAKOTA

MINNESOTA

WISCONSIN

Le Mars

Storm Lake

McGregor

Mason City

Sioux City

Mississippi River

Waterloo

IOWA

Missouri River

Dedham

Maquoketa

Amana

Urbandale

Missouri Valley

Des Moines

80

80

88

NEBRASKA

Indianola

Pella

Council Bluffs

Fort Madison

Blanchard

MISSOURI

ILLINOIS

29

35

OUR TRIP

We visited many amazing places on our trip! We also met a lot of interesting people along the way. Look at the map on the left. Use your finger to trace all the places we have been.

When did Iowa's 1st public library open? See page 8 for the answer.

What Iowa animal is a marsupial? Page 11 has the answer.

When do owls hunt? See page 12 for the answer.

When were the Effigy Mounds built? Look on page 15 for the answer.

How many villages did the Amana community build? Page 21 has the answer.

Who was Carrie Chapman Catt? Turn to page 24 for the answer.

Where can you taste the world's largest raspberry dessert? Look on page 26 for the answer.

How many homes are powered by the Buena Vista County Wind Farm? Turn to page 31 for the answer.

That was a great trip! We have traveled all over Iowa! There are a few places that we didn't have time for, though. Next time, we plan to visit the National Balloon Classic in Indianola. Visitors can ride in a hot-air balloon. You must be at least 6 years old and 4 feet (1 m) tall.

More Places to Visit in Iowa

WORDS TO KNOW

avian (AY-vee-uhn) relating to birds

bluffs (BLUHFS) high, steep banks

colonies (KOL-uh-neez) settlements that often have ties with a mother country

effigy (EF-uh-gee) an image or model of a person or animal

environment (en-VYE-ruhn-muhnt) natural surroundings such as air, water, and soil

heritage (HER-uh-tij) the customs passed on by a group of people over the years

immigrants (IM-uh-gruhnts) people who move to another country

migrating (MYE-grate-ing) traveling to another location as the seasons change

musket (MUHSS-kit) an early type of rifle

prairies (PRAIR-eez) flat or gently rolling lands covered by grasses

traditional (truh-DISH-uhn-uhl) following long-held customs

Iowa covers 55,869 square miles (144,701 sq km). It's the 23rd-largest state in size.

STATE SYMBOLS

State bird: Eastern goldfinch (wild canary)

State flower: Wild rose

State rock: Geode

State tree: Oak

State flag

State seal

STATE SONG

"Song of Iowa"

Words by S. H. M. Byers, sung to the tune of the
traditional Christmas song "O Tannenbaum"

You asked what land I love the best, Iowa, 'tis Iowa,
The fairest State of all the west, Iowa, O! Iowa.
From yonder Mississippi's stream
To where Missouri's waters gleam
O! fair it is as poet's dream, Iowa, in Iowa.

See yonder fields of tasseled corn, Iowa, in Iowa,
Where plenty fills her golden horn, Iowa, in Iowa.
See how her wondrous prairies shine
To yonder sunset's purpling line.
O! Happy land, O! land of mine, Iowa, O! Iowa.

And she has maids whose laughing eyes, Iowa, O! Iowa.
To him whose loves were Paradise, Iowa, O! Iowa.
O! happiest fate that e'er was known.
Such eyes to shine for one alone,
To call such beauty all his own. Iowa, O! Iowa.

Go read the story of thy past, Iowa, O! Iowa.
What glorious deeds, what fame thou hast! Iowa, O! Iowa.
So long as time's great cycle runs,
Or nations weep their fallen ones,
Thou'lt not forget thy patriot sons, Iowa, O! Iowa.

FAMOUS PEOPLE

Beiderbecke, Leon "Bix" (1903–1931), jazz musician

Carothers, Wallace Hume (1896–1937), chemist and inventor

Carson, Johnny (1925–2005), talk show host

Cody, William Frederick "Buffalo Bill" (1846–1917), scout and showman

De Forest, Lee (1873–1961), inventor

Gallup, George H. (1901–1984), pollster

Glaspell, Susan (1876–1948), author

Hoover, Herbert (1874–1964), 31st U.S. president

Landers, Ann (1918–2002), advice columnist

Leahy, William D. (1875–1959), naval officer

Lewis, John L. (1880–1969), labor leader

Martin, Glenn (1886–1955), aircraft manufacturer

Miller, Glenn (1904–1944), bandleader

Rabe, David (1940–), screenwriter and playwright

Reed, Donna (1921–1986), actor

Sunday, Billy (1862–1935), evangelist

Van Allen, James A. (1914–), space scientist

Wayne, John (1907–1979), actor

Williams, Andy (1927–), singer

Wood, Grant (1892–1942), painter

TO FIND OUT MORE

At the Library
Balcavage, Dynise. *Iowa*. New York: Children's Press, 2002.

Horton, Loren. *Uniquely Iowa*. Chicago: Heinemann Library, 2004.

Pierce, Patricia, and Bruce Langton (illustrator). *H Is for Hawkeye: An Iowa Alphabet*. Chelsea, Mich.: Sleeping Bear Press, 2003.

Souter, Gerry, and Janet Souter. *Herbert Hoover, Our Thirty-First President*. Chanhassen, Minn.: The Child's World, 2001.

On the Web
Visit our home page for lots of links about Iowa:
http://www.childsworld.com/links

Note to Parents, Teachers, and Librarians: We routinely verify our Web links to make sure they are safe, active sites—so encourage your readers to check them out!

Places to Visit or Contact
Iowa Tourism Office
200 East Grand Avenue
Des Moines, IA 50309
515/242-4700
For more information about traveling in Iowa

State Historical Society of Iowa
600 East Locust
Des Moines, IA 50319
515/281-5111
For more information about the history of Iowa

INDEX

40

Bye, Hawkeye State.
We had a great time.
We'll come back soon!